Grade K

Scott Foresman

Practice Book 2
Unit 2

PEARSON
Scott Foresman

Editorial Offices: Glenview, Illinois • Parsippany, New Jersey • New York, New York
Sales Offices: Needham, Massachusetts • Duluth, Georgia • Glenview, Illinois
Coppell, Texas • Sacramento, California • Mesa, Arizona

ISBN: 0-328-14510-6

Contents

Unit 2
Animals Live Here

Name _____

✏️ **Write**

_____

- - - - - - - - - - - - - - - - - - - -

_____

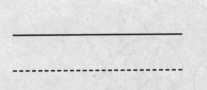

_____

- - - - - - - - - - - - - - - - - - - -

_____

Aa

_____

- - - - - - - - - - - - - - - - - - - -

_____

_____

- - - - - - - - - - - - - - - - - - - -

_____

_____

- - - - - - - - - - - - - - - - - - - -

_____

 Directions: Name each picture. Write *a* on the line if the word begins with /a/. Color the /a/ pictures.

School + Home **Home Activity:** Have your child find other words that begin with /a/.

Name _____

 **Write**  **Color**

| have | is | little | am |

_____

- -

The fish _____ fins.

_____

- -

I ___ am ___ fishing.

_____

- -

The fish is ___ little ___.

_____

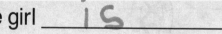

_____

- -

The girl ___ is ___ fishing.

 Directions: Write the missing word to finish each sentence. Color the pictures.

School + Home **Home Activity:** Have your child use the high-frequency words in other sentences.

© Pearson Education K

Name _____

✏️ **Draw**   🖍️ **Color**

~~~~~~

~~~~~~

 Directions: Have children compare and contrast a shark and a goldfish. Draw the bigger animal in the top box and color it. Draw the smaller animal in the bottom box and color it. Tell how the animals are alike and different.

 Home Activity: Have your children explain similarities and differences between a shark and a goldfish.

Practice Book Unit 2

Comprehension Compare and Contrast **7**

Name _____

 Write  Color

1 + 1 = 2

Aa

Directions: Write *a* on a line. Color the pictures with middle /a/.

School + Home **Home Activity:** Find an object at home that begins with *a*. Draw a picture of it and write the word.

Name _____

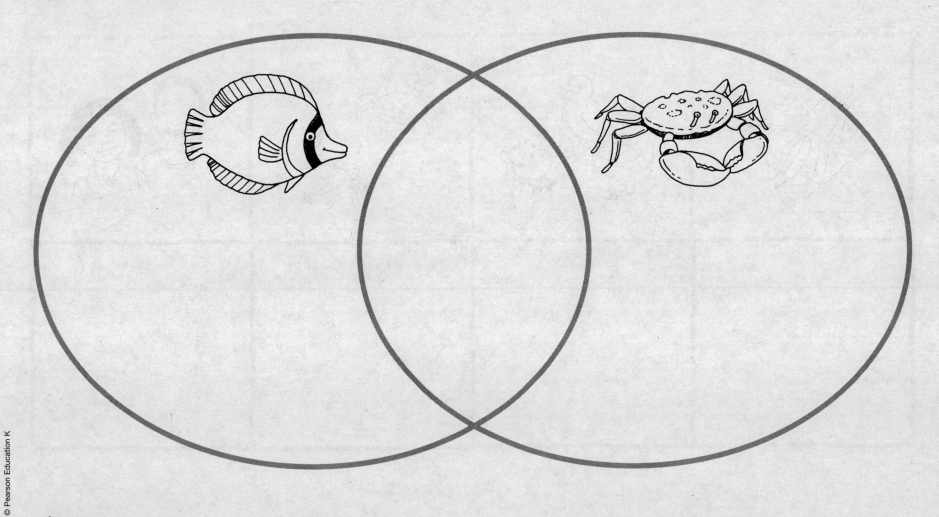

✏ **Write**

 Directions: In the separate circles, draw something that shows how a fish and a crab are different. In the space where the circles overlap, draw a picture that shows how a fish and a crab are alike.

 Home Activity: While you eat a meal together, talk about how the foods are alike and different.

Name _____

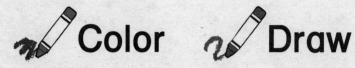 Color  Draw

Directions: Color the pictures. Draw pictures of their homes. Tell what places you drew.

 Home Activity: Discuss the names for different places people or animals live.

Color pictures that begin with /s/.

Family Times

You are your child's first teacher!

This week we're ...

Reading *Armadillo's Orange*

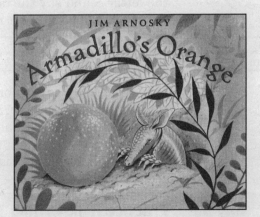

Talking About *Orange Groves*

Learning About Connect /s/ to Ss
Setting

Here are ways to help your child practice skills while having fun!

Day 1 — Read Together

Ask your child to pretend that you are at the beach together. Have him or her name items you would find at the beach that begin with /s/, such as *sun, sand, sunglasses, sandwiches, sailboat.*

Day 2 — Read Together

Have your child read the Phonics Story *Sock Sack.* Find /s/ words.

Day 3 — Connect /s/ to Ss

Review the words that begin with /s/. Write *at* on a piece of paper. Have your child add the letter *s* and say the new word. Write *am*. Have your child add the letter *S* and say the new word. Tell your child that *Sam* is a name so it needs an uppercase *S*.

Day 4 — Proper Nouns

Have your child say his or her name. Ask what school your child goes to. Ask your child the teacher's name. Ask for a friend's name. Tell your child that the words that name specific people and places begin with uppercase letters.

Day 5 — Practice Handwriting

Have your child write his or her name. Check that the letters are formed correctly and that beginning capital letters are used.

2

Words to talk about

armadillo	burrow	tortoise
rattlesnake	grubs	insects

Words to read

have	is	little
am	the	to
sat	Sam	mat

© Pearson Education K

3

Name _____

 Write  Color

_____

- - - - - - - - - - - - - - - -

_____

_____

- - - - - - - - - - - - - - - -

_____

_____

- - - - - - - - - - - - - - - -

_____

Ss

_____

- - - - - - - - - - - - - - - -

_____

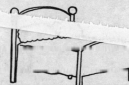

_____

- - - - - - - - - - - - - - - -

_____

_____

- - - - - - - - - - - - - - - -

_____

 Directions: Name each picture. Write *s* on the line if the word begins with /s/. Color the /s/ pictures.

School + Home **Home Activity:** Find pictures that begin with /s/. Paste the pictures on paper to make an /s/ book.

Name

 Write  Color

| have | is |

_____

I _____ to go to school.

_____

This _____ the school.

_____

I _____ to go home.

_____

This _____ home.

Directions: Write the missing word to finish each sentence. Color the pictures.

Home Activity: Use *have* and *is* in other sentences.

14 **High-Frequency Words**

Practice Book Unit 2

© Pearson Education K

I have the sock.

© Pearson Education K

Sock Sack

I have a sack.

The sock sack is little.

The sock is little.

Name _____

 Color  Draw

© Pearson Education K

 Directions: Color the pictures. Then draw a picture that tells setting of the story in the last box.

 Home Activity: Draw a picture of the setting for one of your favorite stories.

Name _____

 Write  Color

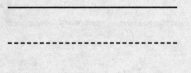

Ss

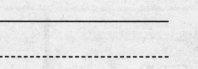

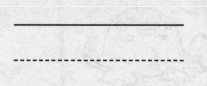

 Directions: Write *s* if the word ends with /s/. Color the picture if the word begins with /s/.

School + Home **Home Activity:** Find an object that begins with the letter *s*. Draw a picture of it and write the word.

18 **Phonics** Consonant *Ss*/s/

Practice Book Unit 2

Name _____

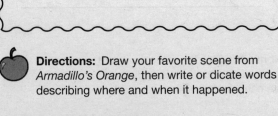 Draw ✏️ Write

Directions: Draw your favorite scene from *Armadillo's Orange*, then write or dicate words describing where and when it happened.

 Home Activity: Talk about or look at photographs of a favorite event. Discuss where and when it happened.

Name _____

 Draw 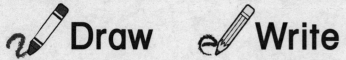 Write

 Directions: Draw a pet you know, a friend, and a relative. Write or dictate their names.

 Home Activity: Write the names of everyone in your family. Talk about how people's first and last names are capitalized.

Name _____

 Write  Color

_____
- - - - - - - - - - - - - - - -
_____

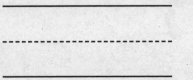

_____
- - - - - - - - - - - - - - - -
_____

Pp

_____
- - - - - - - - - - - - - - - -
_____

_____
- - - - - - - - - - - - - - - -
_____

_____
- - - - - - - - - - - - - - - -
_____

© Pearson Education K

 Directions: Name each picture. Write *p* on the line if the word begins with /p/. Color the picture.

School + Home **Home Activity:** Find pictures that begin with /p/. Paste the pictures on paper to make a /p/ book.

Name _____

 **Write**  **Color**

| we | my | like |

_____
- - - - - - - - - - - - - - - - - - -
We _____ the cat.

_____
- - - - - - - - - - - - - - - - - - -
We _____ my dog.

_____
- - - - - - - - - - - - - - - - - - -
_____ like to tap.

_____
- - - - - - - - - - - - - - - - - - -
_____ pig is little.

Directions: Write the missing word to finish each sentence. Color the pictures.

 Home Activity: Use *we*, *my*, and *like* in other sentences.

© Pearson Education K

Name _____

 Color

Directions: Look at the story. Color the picture that tells the main idea.

 Home Activity: Talk about stories and have children tell the main idea of each story.

Name _____

Name _____

 Color    Write

_____

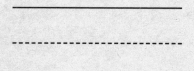

_____

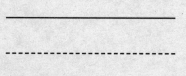

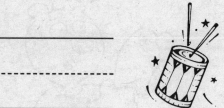

Pp

_____

_____

_____

Directions: Write *p* on the line if the word ends with /p/. Color the final /p/ words.

School + Home   **Home Activity:** Have your child use the words in sentences.

Name _____

Draw

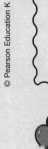
Directions: Draw a picture to show the main idea of
the story *Animal Babies in Grassland.*

Home Activity: Ask your child to tell you about the
main idea in the story *Animal Babies in Grasslands.*

Name _____

Write

Directions: Have children look at the picture and write the child's name on the line.

Home Activity: Show pictures to your child and have him or her name the people in the pictures.

© Pearson Education K

We like the caps.

Phonics Story *The Cap*
Target Skill Consonant Cc/k/

The Cap

I have a cap.

The cap is my cap.

I like my cap.

2

Name _____

 Write  Color

 Directions: Label the animal in each picture R for *real* or M for *make-believe*. Color the pictures that show a make-believe setting.

 Home Activity: Draw and color a picture of a real animal in a real setting.

Name _____

 Write  Color

_____

- - - - - - - - - - - - - - - - - -

_____

_____

- - - - - - - - - - - - - - - - - -

_____

Cc

_____

- - - - - - - - - - - - - - - - - -

_____

_____

- - - - - - - - - - - - - - - - - -

_____

_____

- - - - - - - - - - - - - - - - - -

_____

_____

- - - - - - - - - - - - - - - - - -

_____

 Directions: Name each picture. Write *c* on the line if the word begins with /k/. Color the /k/ pictures.

 Home Activity: Have your child find other words that begin with /k/.

38 **Phonics** Consonant *Cc* /k/

Name _____

 Circle  Color

 Directions: Circle the make-believe pictures. Color the real pictures.

 Home Activity: With your child, look at a book about how real animals live.

© Pearson Education K

Name _____

 Draw  Color

2 red balls

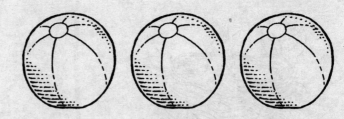

4 blue balls

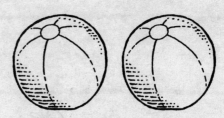

3 yellow balls

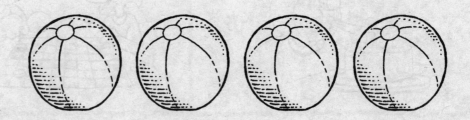

 Directions: Match the words to the pictures. Color the balls.

School + Home **Home Activity:** Have your child name adjectives (color, size, number) for items around the house.

40 **Grammar** Adjectives

Name _____

 **Color**   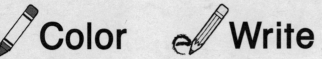 **Write**

_____
- - - - - - - - - - - - - - - - - -
_____

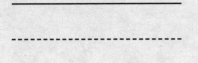

_____
- - - - - - - - - - - - - - - - - -
_____

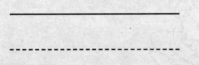

_____
- - - - - - - - - - - - - - - - - -
_____

Ii

_____
- - - - - - - - - - - - - - - - - -
_____

_____
- - - - - - - - - - - - - - - - - -
_____

_____
- - - - - - - - - - - - - - - - - -
_____

 Directions: Name each picture. Write _i_ on the line if the word begins with /i/. Color the _i_ words.

 School + Home **Home Activity:** Look through a newspaper or book with your child and point out words that begin with _Ii_.

Name _____

 Write  Color

```
he      for
```

_____

- - - - - - - - - - - - - - - - - -

_____ has a pan.

_____

- - - - - - - - - - - - - - - - - -

The pan is _____ for you.

_____ likes the pan.

_____

- - - - - - - - - - - - - - - - - -

It is _____ Pam.

Directions: Write the missing word to finish each sentence. Color the pictures.

School + Home **Home Activity:** Write the words *he* and *for* using a fun material (yarn, sticks, glitter).

Name _____

 Color

 Directions: Color the picture that shows what comes first in each story.

© Pearson Education K

 Home Activity: Draw three pictures to show how to feed a pet.

Name _____

 Trace  Color

wet

old

empty

full

dry

young

Directions: Trace the words. Color the pictures.

 Home Activity: Say one of the words on the page and ask your child to tell you its opposite.

50 **Grammar** Adjectives

© Pearson Education K

Sit, pat, sip.

Phonics Story *Sam Can!*
Target Skill Short *Ii/i/*

Sam Can!

Sam can sit.

Sam can pat.

Sam can sip.

Name _____

 Color

Directions: Color the pictures that show something real.

Home Activity: Draw a picture of a real garden.

Practice Book Unit 2

Comprehension Realism and Fantasy **57**

Name _____

 Write  Color

_____
- -
_____

_____
- -
_____

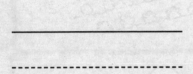

_____
- -
_____

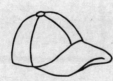

 Ii

_____
- -
_____

_____
- -
_____

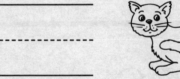

_____
- -
_____

 Directions: Name the pictures. Write *i* on the lines if the word has middle /i/. Color the /i/ pictures.

School + Home **Home Activity:** Have your child draw a picture of something with /i/.

Name _____

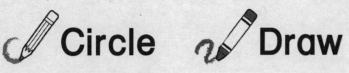 Circle   Draw

 Directions: Color the picture that shows something make-believe. Draw something real in the box.

 Home Activity: Read a favorite story together and talk about whether the story is make-believe or something that could really happen.

Practice Book Unit 2

Comprehension Realism and Fantasy **59**

Name _____

 **Draw**

big

big

little

little

🍎 **Directions:** Draw lines to match the adjective with the pictures.

School + Home **Home Activity:** Ask your child to name the color, shape, or size of articles around the house.

60 Grammar Adjectives

Practice Book Unit 2